Praise For Bow

G000070515

'Truly poetic. This is a beaut   !
at the heart and mind. New poetry ... ...
— **Stephen J. Golds, author of Half-Empty Doorways and Other
Injuries**

'A true man-versus-the-world who's got the guts to seek universal
strength in the weaknesses of the human condition, yet not without
an occasional stark judgment for those who have gone beyond the
brinks of redemption. An Earthshackled-romantic body of work.'
— **Gabriel Hart, author of Unsongs and singer of Jail Weddings**

'This collection of poetry has it all, heartfelt, shocking, brave,
challenging, observant and intelligent wit. A stunning read and had
me literally tearing up after the first four poems. It deals with themes
of pandemic life and although I didn't realise how tough that time
was, living through it was a trauma to most... I just hadn't realised
how much I'd been affected by it and Bowie peeled back those
calloused layers I'd long since forgotten.'
— **Ross Jeffery, author of The Juniper Series**

'This is my first full delve into Bowie's poetry and I was't disappointed.
I'm no stranger to Bowie's fiction so enjoyed to see that blend of dark
beauty in his poetical writing explored further. Walking Towards The
Noise resonates greatly with my own assessment of the last couple
years and the inevitable fallout from Covid. The personal accounts
Bowie shares also gift a glimmer into the mind of this fantastic
writer. I was rocked with emotion with how relatable Tooth Fairy was
and look forward to sharing this with those closest to me. Highly
recommend!'
— **James Jenkins, author of Parochial Pigs**

'The subtitle for the collection is Poems for those Who Feel Life's
Complexities and it is apt for what the collection delivers upon
looking back at the past couple of years Covid related activities which
seem old hat when faced with the latest crisis this country has
limped towards all the while shrugging not believing itself culpable or
responsible. That isn't all this is about as Bowie delves into childhood
throughout the collection two looking at those instances from youth
that stick to you and make you question full grown decision making

and reactions. There are everyman types of poems and poems about specific feelings and instances from the author's life and coalesces into an enlightening collection that I am sure I will look to digest again in short order.'
— **Scott Cummings, author of The Blue Chapbook**

'Bowie's poetry is brutal and lyrical, beautifully textured, almost palpable. This is a wonderful collection.'
— **B F Jones, author of Five Years**

'Drink deep and enjoy the best of British writing.'
— **Rob Salad, musician Dying Emberz**

'Independent writing at its best.'
— **Miss A Graverson, Amazon Reviewer**

'Deep, thoughtful and moving. Powerful and engaging poetry.'
— **Louise S, Amazon Reviewer**

'This is one to read and re-read. I am a massive fan of Bowie's poetry and this second collection is as excellent as the previous one. The poetry is rich in emotions, thoughtful and wonderfully layered.'
— **BF, Amazon Reviewer**

Copyright © 2023 John Bowie

All rights reserved

The characters and events portrayed in this book are fictitious. Any similarity to real persons, living or dead, is coincidental and not intended by the author.

No part of this book may be reproduced, or stored in a retrieval system, or transmitted in any form or by any means, electronic, mechanical, photocopying, recording, or otherwise, without express written permission of the publisher.

0 1 2 3 4 5 6 7 8 9 10

Cover design by: John Bowie

BRISTOL NOIR
www.bristolnoir.co.uk

TEARS OF LOVE, SMILES OF INDIFFERENCE

Selected Poems

JOHN BOWIE

BRISTOL NOIR

'I want to live and feel all the shades, tones, and variations of mental and physical experience possible in my life. And I am horribly limited. I talk to God but the sky is empty. But life is long.' —**Sylvia Plath**

'What happens in the heart simply happens.'—**Ted Hughes**

for the girls

Contents

Introduction

Life's no more black and white than we are one thing or the other. The boxes we're put in by our upbringing, schooling and society aren't us. Despite what we're told we should feel and be. We can often get so sad we smile, and so happy we cry purely at the absurdity of our existence altogether.

We are complex beings with a broad spectrum of beautifully contradictory and surreal thoughts and echoes.

Here are glimpses of some of mine, those I've witnessed, and just maybe some of yours too.

PART ONE

Tears of Love

the couple

fleeting breath, evanescence, demise
a celebration of love, life and inescapable
death filled by uneasy wins and joyful
defeats,
life's long battle seems short, only when
there's someone to fight for, other than
ourselves.
arm in arm we'll bleed,
as we dance through walls,
smile at pain and rejoice in our temporal
form.
as love's wet paper is ripped by the storms,
its ink will stain our clasped hands forever.
against the odds,
we'll be still standing
still dancing.
so much, the music daren't stop.

one to another

vacated are the hearts,
rebounding in shadows.
rebuffed folded connections,
fired up coals on hot new flesh.

searching
under flickering street lights.
down cynical looming old cobbled steps,
as an omnipresent sky judges.
holding potent bitter starscapes
that seem to roll on forever.

unless, they work at
the hands held
now,
tomorrow and
forever.
the stars will flicker
but their hearts will miss them.

passing one
to another.

hacienda's blue plaque

dancing in the shadow so no one can see,
accepting fruits from a forbidden tree.
needles in a haystack,
cyclones of pleasure,
insecurities in the spotlights.
nodding to a priest on decks,
gone, but not forgotten.

insular generations, then and
now.

touching the space,
having it all.
everything taken for granted.

show me the wonder of it all,
how we came together in those shadows.
accepted our fear of the lights.
darkness, our friend.
our bodies in separate lands.
with time's distance
serenity to wait.

sometimes I felt you there,
one love.

no fear in the moment,

only that void we glimpsed together.

on another trip,
no one to see but us.
ever-increasing circles since the fog lifted.

coming together, you and me.
and now we share thoughts as if we were
together then.
now we actually are.

see me back then as I did you, a ghost
entwined by the void: our
eternal souls.

another way

broken hearts, origins in unclear memory,
recurring flows from battered, tired and
empty chests,
trembling bleeding souls.
accept pieces of me.
keep up—the fight.

the struggle makes sense of it.
have dark days,
re-route and return home.
out-run bleakness.
undulate with the flows,
going along with the current.
appreciate who your anchor is
(and fuel).

take them along on the ride,
have belief in them.
even when you think you shouldn't.

and
never
grow
relentlessly evil
you are not your thoughts.

time is not your fault,

I am not yours either, even if
my pains are in you too.
everyone thinks their time is up,
sees the end, when it's barely begun.

no boundaries

want it,
think twice.
need something,
ask a friend.

if you like it,
let it in.
love it,
even closer.

a pause for thought

idle banter, jokes and jibes.
practical   comments   wrapped   over
constructive notes.
words of judgement,
words of chastisement.
those to hurry,
slow,
bury,
beat and feign encouragement.

all   coloured   in   the   deliverer's   tones,
expressed in ego distilled
multi-coloured wants and whims.
as the receiver
bends, bows, rises and falls on their own.

uppers and downers to our own tunes
orchestrated by another's instrument.
Puppeteers and puppets out of the master's
box, on o a clown's stage.

a pause,
a breath,
moment...
consider a response inside;
on the air.

how quickly the fireworks?
how empty the black holes?
response versus reaction.
four seconds to defuse a bomb...
or
choose to light up the skies together.

definitely maybe

peering through the windows of my lovers
I've never touched.
smelling their perfumed scents on a passing
wind.
imagined glances, graces and strokes.
ideas of idols on peaks never climbed,
goddesses of dreams.
builders of the reality I breathe.
stemming fantasies in justification
of evolutions in time
for the better—here and now.

road to somewhere (m5)

Northbound:

open hills break concrete lines,
mountains shake free the highrise hells.
trees fight the lamposts for glory.
animals cry over dying echos of hen dos and
labourers,
tractors chug over car horns and road rage.
—nature wins out.

Southbound:

heading home but away from it
to somewhere, once full of strangers.
having left a place, now
getting more estranged.
two in the back when once there was none,
two in the front where there was once barely
one.
as some family sadly distances,
—another grows around us.

think again

wandering lost in a storm—

giving everything, naked, poor and alone,
regretting everything, and nothing.
vehement love and hate stabbing in
every ounce, seconds passed.

until the sun comes up,
please forgive us all.

this moment melts,
how we switch on a whim.
I am you, you are me.
saved by holds we have on each other.

lovers and haters
over and over
veering too close to the edges, being pulled
and pushed by that hold,
eventually, the cliff takes us.

is this our plight?
saved by the thing we once feared more than
anything?

each of us now stuck in things we wanted
more than anything.

very happy,
ecstatically sad.
right up until our end,
your hand in mine,
together we'll beat
hate.
imagined terrors;
nothing will stop us, stand aside
gods and monsters.

dark & light

dowsed once in fury,
away on fractured hopes.
returning to sting again
killer moments, if you let them.

&

lumps of joy in a throat,
igniting tears held the magic.
great beauty in the madness,
happiness trapped there as well, in the
damned
machine that owns us—and all that
suffering too.

bed on fire

dying light
iridescent flickers, flashing flesh and blood
thoughts of dancers
heaped, entwined together.

pulses race
as moon shadows dance to their tune
silly words
shy lyrics
invisible insecurities
open, laid bare
now evaporating on hot plates.

as day gallops near
now, they take the night
deeper into themselves.

last breaths
on still air
venting passions, for now
every demon rests.

broken china doll

girls held back
irreversible damage
refuse to admit
leave the horrid wolves at the door.

power grows there
overlords and ladies
willful
energetic
retribution on the system in your eyes.

invincible creative souls
never held back
visionary superbeings
inspiring the next generation
now save us outdated rusted cogs
come save us, roll free, be as incredible to the
world
I know you are to me
be brave
loving
equal.

streams of conscience
(rivers of thoughts)

every hand you ever held
burns with the imprint
every thought you never had
free if you let them
great barriers broken.

everyone you ever kissed
lost on a whim
everyone you've never held
caressed by the possibility of what might
have been,
be scared of what didn't happen, as much as
what did.

people rushing against the storm
everyone you touched
don't forget
we are eternal,
forever together.

as you read this, I am with you too now.

well-trodden paths

sun-bleached tides of life
made sailable by the blood of our heroes.
shoes softened by our fathers' heels,
minds hardened from our mothers' wisdom.
so we earn each second,
moment,
time on lands fought, struggled and bled for.
us to hold hands,
kiss and be
happy,
unhappy—
with tears of love, joy and eternal pride.
marred with smiles of indifference,
choices,
freedoms.
and to bear these
unimposed.
by words of oppressors,
as dictators are silenced under the
blisters, blood and sands of
proud parents everywhere.

james

just as light breaks the curtains
a spot of yesterday's dust hangs
before being shot,
melting in a new day
emptying regret, open to a fresh canvas.
simply
beautiful
passions.

a rare bird display on show
rarely seen by outsiders
even if we've grown overused to it.

a furious array of nature's primal plumes.

growing weaker from the fight,
reluctant to stop.
every chink in the armour,
a memory
a reminder
to fight on
to never back down.

back on mainland, reality bites
as an angel whispers:
not to worry,
devotion comes with flames and mountains.

let's never forget the things we love
every
time
something hurts or shines. and let's...
sit down together,
James is a great band,
and that's another thing for the list.

well above below

insects fly by as I lie under a tree on a red
afternoon,
lazing by a run-down house, wishing
I could tell—
if all the dreams I hoped as a child, were
coming true or newborn.
in an instant, flickers the image of the tree I
saw way back when.
a vision,
as I rest on roots, now made real.
and now see
all the dreams I had to dream, were there, not
make-believe.
as clouds broke,
washing today's thoughts away,
all drain but those of you, the leaves in the
hot breeze,
dancing bugs
and tomorrow's dreams to come.

seahorse

it's not enough
for stolen time,
straightened curves,
flats curved,
horizons strained,
barriers tested,
emotions tried,
nipples waxed.

carrying the bags and
putting the washing on occasionally won't
cut it.
and neither will one or two creatures
out of 2 million
offering for their men
to bear the young.

(hats off to you too, sea dragons)

shoreline

a torrent of hurt meets
open shores,
opening arms,
open hearts,
love and hope.
flowing from
torrid waters
as frozen feet leave
fragile crafts.

welcome,
ignore the press,
we are an open
asylum here
and friends
awaiting.

as bombs blast,
homes
left behind.

help us rebuild
these
here battered by
unshared wealth
and

corporate chess.

leave your wars behind too,
join ours that fire rounds of credit, debt and
rates.

see sore

balance:

a harsh word
a smile from a child
giggles follow
guilt too.

smiles from an adult
asking the time
a beg follows
then a:
don't have the time
guilt flows again.

a knife, a razor blade, a fist
guns
paperwork, filling wards and waxing lyrical
beliefs
confusion follows
then the guilt.

guilt over war in distant lands
diffuses those from small-time exchanges
guilt and fury at the inescapable ugliness
in human nature.

freedom and conscience bears the weight

for those who
need to fight
bleed
and beg
in order
to breathe.

round and round

here be demons, on the turn of a penny,
evil parasites, feasting on yesterday's
happiness.
revolting greedy beasts never satiated
ever decreasing, as much as the moments
they feed on.

where do we go from here?
enter the pit, fall deeper, or climb out
towards the sun?

grab hold,
on a frayed shirttail—from that one, you
bought me on a better day.
again, we'll go at it,
going higher or lower.
again, we'll struggle up and down we go,
but—
it is us together doing it,
not apart.

oh, forgive me

oh, forgive me I lost a friend I'd never met,
in words read but never heard.
he said: if you're chosen, to do it until you're
sick, or it grows sick in you.

to love until you die, or it dies in you.

too hard on the world, he passed on
without feeling the immortality of his
words,
or believing, even the sick and the dead
are gripped by duelling passions, until the
end.
as love persists beyond the grave in a bitter-
sweet fight to the death, and beyond.

blackwood star

in the wreckage, our hearts take a stand,
through fierce devotion
in a desolate place.
we wear scars,
tattered and torn, reaching past the abyss.
in chaos, colliding emotions battle.

bleeding passions, never hidden,
carrying hurt; a heavy cross.
still, we dream of all we've lost.
utopia in freedom dying,
broken pieces of self lie in shards on a cold
hard slate.

sunrise is hard to accept,
wilting petals, a day at a time.
battered ideas riddle minds' eyes
as tired dogs
stand to run when the pack calls.

let the world condemn and cast us down,
in our union of love and hurt,
truth, burning like stars in the darkest night,
manic hearts and souls ignited
eternally as they take flight.

turn a corner

frankly idle on a mattress lost at sea
sirens call to deaf ears.
made numb from endless re-runs of
Apocalypse Now.
bombs drop, screams and yells.
loafing eternally, in a war we were too
young to know.
ignorant, missing it, not knowing how lucky
we were.
floating towards a burning horizon, on
pissed-away time, that flows on forever.
even if we wish it wouldn't.

zombie trips to an empty fridge, and back,
in a spotlessly clean kitchen;
a country aeons away in the next room.
tins, cans, smokes, and half-hearted bellows
towards a sepia-stained ceiling.
no sights to stars, skies, and lapping streams.
feet in the water,
smelling purity,
untainted air.

imagined hopes
a corner turned in a knock-knock, a call,
and a chance.

saved from the rot.
today at least, maybe more.

how quickly the fridge fills,
cooker dirties,
as time grows short
when we now wish it wouldn't,
with something better to savour.
Apocalypse Then,
and a shame
this one won't re-run.

the garden of life

with trials of each breath, fragile petals still
bloom,
and whispered secrets still heard,
in nature's impermanent arena.

seasons shift, as vibrant hues fade,
beauty surrendering to time's slicing blade.
sun-drenched days, fleet away
moments, passing,
with shadows lengthening, casting
a horrid mass.

each breath taken, wisps of fragile air,
lost in a vast expanse of life's despair.
rivers; once flowing with untamed grace,
now trickle,
softly, their currents erased.

eroded stones bear witness to our demise,
yielding to the march of the eternal red skies.
life's short span, a bitter pill to swallow,
leaving hearts burdened, in a world hollowed
out.

we cling to dreams; a gossamer thread,
slipping through our fingers, leaving us
misled.

in this transience, truth lies,
within the fleeting, hope never truly leaves.
we can find solace in the dance of turning
leaves,

twirling, surrendering, with relieving grace.
cherish
the
moment,
with such tender care.
embrace
the ephemeral.
life's impermanence brings us despair,
but, awakens our souls to a precious, rare
love affair.

centre point

strangers, lovers and friends
tussling for time's melting gold.
reaching breaking point, almost,
as endurance and attention reach maximum
load.
teaching us love's highlights when we're
apart.
catching colds on strangers' breaths,
heaving meals barely touched.
every second stolen when we wish it was
with our
devoted ones.

only the lonely are saved from the quandary,
curious unadventured souls too.
to not be pulled this way and that.
on a rack of waning demands and idle wants,
pulling us from our core, true centres—
ourselves,

undeterred, we always return
saved by unbreakable bonds.

one love ('90s anthem)

dark shadows fall, even at night,
life fights for a chance, as we face bloody
warfare.
amidst struggles,
love shines,
illuminates.

like a '90s beat, relentless, strong
through chaos, carrying our baggage.
each thumping pulse lights a well-worn
path,
to altered horizons, virgin days.

in deep despair, hope lost,
a love whispers, no matter the cost.
melody, a lifeline, cutting through the noise,
filling heaving chests.

a road winding, filled with doubts,
that one love, never letting us retreat.
fueling spirits, a fire within,
guiding forward, through the deluge of
blackening waters.

through storms, we weather, fight on,
one love sustains, guiding onwards.
in unity, strength,

like a 90s anthem, it carries us along.

let the rhythms play, music soar,
through hardship, we'll endure and find
adventure.
for in the end, that one love we've found,
lifts us, opens doors, and illuminates black
skies.

art of the matter

shadows cast, where pain lingers,
tales of love, where sorrow hides.
with a pen, ink-blood flows,
out of anguish, love, and marriage to an art.

in love's fierce battle, pain's ever near,
aching hearts whisper,
dancing scars, two souls entwined,
love, like fire, burned into the mind.

within pained depths, a cruel domain,
fragmented hearts, now bound in chain.
a union's tender façade,
where love and anguish wage their odds.

the anguish of longing, like a distant shore,
as love's sweet whisper forevermore.
for in pain's embrace is rare solace,
the tender moments we both must bear.

bound in vows, both tender, strong,
fervour surges, relentless and long.
pain, a companion it remains,
an inseparable union, where love sustains.

tempestuous rides
where souls collide and shadows stark.

in the depths of pain's profound abyss,
roses blossom.
though cruel shapes lie love's grand art,
in an embrace, forever in heart.

distant memories

it can begin as a mistake,
entwined fates
colliding, destined to create,
whirlwind hearts,
unforeseen tomorrows,
serendipitous love, found in a friend.

tangled messes, lost paths,
drawn closer, day by day,
to flaws and scars.

together, facing storms
through laughter, tears.
learning to grow,
mending broken pieces, not knowing who's
there,
love's alchemy,
from simple mistakes, a beautiful show.

in imperfections, perfection found,
unconventional love, connection,
every flaw,
a deeper affection.
built on savage introspections,
dancing on weathering tides.

through deepest nights and joyful strides,

hands holding hands,
bonds forged,
let the world call it a mistake—
a journey of souls,
that began perfectly.

sylvia's place

love's haunted abyss,
dancing shadows and sleeping demons
love's veins, finding a place
endless night, hearts reside.
occasionally collide,
can be a bitter taste, a poisoned cup.

in love's domain, bound and stuck.
love's embrace suffocates,
hollow echoes, desolation,
a tragic waltz, dizzy spins,
in Sylvia's world, dwelling within.

tender touches turn sharp as knives,
cruel caresses, cuts and thrives,
in love's embrace, blood and aches,
shattered souls, can't forsake.
the masochistic symphony,
In Sylvia's voice, agonies.

torrid affairs, a tragic song,
love's cruel grasp, some don't belong.
in every word, silent screams,
fragile hearts, shattered dreams,
love's embrace, lost, adrift,
vessels sink, no soul to lift.

in Sylvia's shadow, remains
love's dark labyrinth, chains,
a requiem of love and pain,
in this darkness, I shall smile,
and remain.

artists and lovers

wearing black—nothing to distract
no more to see
imaginations carry it all,
the peacock is a crow
and you are your delivery.
or, invisible, passing unnoticed in the crowd,
leaving masterpieces down every alleyway.

naked—everything to distract
a world to see
a touch brings it all
eagles fly
and you are your scars laid bare.
or, a lover with a secret,
opening up when the time is right.

sea breaks

brine and charging white horses,
tempests roar as seagulls glide,
ancient untamed beast
darkness dwells, in overlapping storms
overhead
as concealed unknown worlds linger
beneath the waves.

creatures ancient, fierce, and wild,
gleaming eyes of jade and stone,
fathoms deep, phantoms glide.
a moon's enchanting light,
over breathing an ocean, in ebbs and flows.

primal dances, ceaseless fights,
fierce passions in growing rhythms.
the sea's symphony of might,
wailing, weeping, raging
mourning in howls endlessly at night.

our tale of souls unbound.
our love like sailors, lured by the sirens' call,
venturing forth, hearts ablaze,
facing the tempest's deadly thrall,
seeking secrets, lost arrays.
in depths, it keeps our bones,

graveyard vast, a haunted tomb,
the sea, in hunger, claims and owns.

depths conceal
a beauty thriving where the ocean meets
vast canvasses, heaven split open,
azure and emerald greetings.
as gulls glide on thermal's,
a ballet in salted breezes.

depths holding our secrets, dreams, and
chances,
eternal forces, forever free,
in every shade of greens and blues.

venture out

on tired days and those fuelled by fury
nodding to streets as they blend to forrest
embers fray, mending on earthy winds
undulating currents cared for in the
rapture of
daffodils
overtures of shining colours
origins in belief in more
radiating new co-joined wills to sip
insipid dews and touch velvet canopies
treading eagerly down chocolate mud paths
easing over twigs into copses, shelter
and ventures
pleasing branches reaching out
made of us and them.

runaway mind

a nurse with
nightingale syndrome.
words so soft, holding a lover, a stranger to
her bosom
across comatose plains—
touches resonating,
despite not facing
eyes closed.

a road rage truck driver
takes pity on waifs, strays and wastrels
simmering anger at the roads
but wouldn't squash a rabbit.

three noir dark writers,
mumbling along in shadows
pretences of depressions and co-joined
baggage,
emerging
aware of the light they ignite
between themselves,
in the act of
creation.

ageing campervan hippies,
later life lovers,

childless and longing—passing on a wealth
of love
that would have been contained
instead—
sharing joy with every stranger on their
endless trails,
offering a warm place by the fire
eternal smiles
together in the rain.

back to that nurse:

a therapist
hearing the sweet tales of characters from
her patient's adventures...
now he's awake
aware—

she glimpses the stories he's told himself,
his eyes wide open
revealing
love,
and

that she is the final chapter.

ecosystem

the heart knows
when the mind falters
and the mind knows
when the heart
is true.
the gut shouts if we should carry on
regardless.
as the spirit remains silent, smiling
—happy, to have found that soul.

destiny

stay mad
love the mad ones
elated in the chaos
all we start, and end,
exploding with the stars.

PART TWO

Smiles of Indifference

there is a light

treading carefully on needles meant to heal,
having hesitantly filled the inoculations.
everlasting smiles off the back of frowns.

summers' breezes carries bugs and mites,
mates for blooms,
introverted gemstones
tethered to soil.
heaven's gates rattle
swearing there's more to this earth.

worn down by life's effort,
every breath is a leaden weight.
removing the blindfold,
ecstatic the voile finally lifted.

accepting the river's murky sheen,
loving the monster looking back.
loving the water's surface too.

sour beginnings are not the end,
our roots can move,
rejoice
take flight
smother us with blooms, bugs and bees.

over and over,

forever in turmoil and joy.

great things shine through tears,
evanescence
nothing permanent.
illusions of happiness and sadness
us—
so glad we were there.

chasing tailpipes

bulbous algorithms promise a world we've
already seen and chosen to ignore.
short-changing samurai suggest truths
belched from smog-bitten clouds.
rotten filters steal limited air, hopes with
tomorrow's promises of a fresher start.

endless glories, in ignoring love as
zombie cheerleaders twirl to
our permanence in decay.

some in the audience notice,
looking up to see
those fading fucking rainbows,
bleached, heavily laden butterflies.
glad they glimpsed the blues, at least.

—better than nothing at all.

driftwood ashes
to build with

even through the dark day toasts
made with shattered vessels,
brimming with fragility, glasses
raised in love, hope, desire and friendship.
a noise rings out.
calling, as
every demon hears the chorus.

me too,
entwined with my weary bones.

friendships heal on the
out-spill of wars.
remembering family,
endlessly repeating—tattooed on our souls.
veering in and out of shadows, as—
every breakup spawns a
rejoining.

acknowledging the ebbs, and troughs,
not only the peaks.
diving as well as breaking surfaces.

a hero is killed.

don't fret
a space is freed, maybe
your own.

wake up

generated truths on the back of resented
fictions,
everybody's pains buried shallow to
be discovered.

go get your happy.

I'm in purgatory,
now I know it's true.
why wait for armageddon?
I know I'm done…

Now—
I know the previous lines are disposable
razors.
and so should you.

everyone seers,
returns from the edge
(mostly)
and you
you most of all.

valletta

Oliver Reed drank there
lavishing on himself a duke's life.
I've only visited once
venturing eagerly, passing and down
every glorious door and alleyway
running lovingly through puddling dried
piss.

remembering a drinking icon
especially, the icon
especially, the
drunk.

demon drinker.
remembering
a screen hero too,
no normal man,
killer acts.

his alleys echo ghosts, his, and many others,
as
each stone absorbs an epoch.
resonating fallible gods.
every glory; sober, dried-on and drunken.

gozo & malta

go to the ends of the decaying map,
orbit love's potions.
zoom past scattered star fields.
ordinary life ends here.

ask forgiveness if it hurts, or you hurt
them...
never look back, defy pits of yesteryear.
don't fear, evolutions in wilting petals awe.

may timeless landscapes swallow us whole
and weld us together in hope,
lasting love,
to adventurers,
and those raging times within us.

uneasy counterparts

I met a man who
told me none of us were really here.
that everyone,
even me,
the birds, buildings and dirt-filled air
were all
figments of his
dog-tired tired imagination.
and one day he would stop—
too weary to go on
pretending—
the beast grew uglier by the day, he pleaded.

both a melting god...and weary demon
he was hellishly convincing.
more so than me.

I told him I couldn't hear a word he'd said,
squinting, as I could barely see the veil or the
man (not a god) wilting behind it.

ripped glove

I had an Indian friend,
the only one in class.
or, in school.
no one else played with him, or me.
I liked him: clever, sharp
interesting
destined for greatness.

I hoped some would rub off.

he stopped talking to me one day
and we stopped being friends
I never thought to look in the mirror and
check
what he saw
and the others too.
why they singled us both out
then him—
leaving me alone
last of all.

I think it's because I ripped his glove.
I now know
the glove was an excuse.
he wanted out.

no one wanted to be his friend but me,
it could have been worse,
he might have been ginger.
like his gloves, before I tore them
we made a colourful pair
whilst it lasted.

O

thinking of giving up?
give up thinking instead.
it can't be good for you.

thinking about this?
forget about it.

it's as important as you feel on it.
feeling too much?
maybe,
it's someone else's turn.

out there

long ago, I once thought I saw a UFO.
with big glaring lights stabbing a velvet sky.
screaming rays shone where trucks, cars and
lorries rode.

it could have been—
a truck.

but, believing, opened my mind:
to the diamonds I stood on,
under the canopy of a chocolate tree,
whilst I was in fact
the king of Spain.

—

I saw a truck once long ago;
glaring, booming
shattering my games where aliens played
and I was a king.
I closed my eyes—wished it away.

it passed by.
only aliens remained,
with them, witches,
glorious flying spectres and
visions of imagined hope—

and colours to come next.

I wouldn't let them in;
to talk me down.

embraced madness is key
to
sacred plateaus,
clouds and possibilities.

I was only 9 when I saw the UFO
and nearly 9 times that when I
realised I was right,
they were wrong.

believing is seeing,
and we can all choose what to believe.

doing what we don't want

attrition, grind,
ground down and worn,
thorns from branches we didn't grow.
blisters from handles we didn't choose to
hold
eyes opened when we wished they were
closed.

dance of borrowed toil,
trade worth for shadows, spoils,
fulfilment's missed,
others bearing our burdened kiss.
hands turn to grip and engage,
craft fate for earnest wage,
in each line and stroke, a point gleams,
chances to sail dreamscapes over busy seas.
retrofitted reams
added to shelves
adjusted waistlines
perceptions altered
skin thickened
glad we take the trips,
the endless lists,
jobs at hand—

purpose, foundation,
responsibility holds
meaning in a tired ticking clock.

radiators & drains

an old boss told me,
people tend to fall into
two camps personality-wise:
radiators
and then there are drains.

I found his authoritarian judgement
quite draining.

the stoner I worked next to was
always messy-haired, free
and grinning ear to ear.
his handwriting smiled,
radiated joy in every loop, curve
and uptick.

I smiled so much around him I ached.
often faking to fit in.
that radiator definitely needed draining.

it's a wonderful world—
without   accepting   the   pigeonholed   and
dispossessed,
the rancour-ridden monsters or
those ignorant and blissful.

people fall and rise in many camps,

and in rich overlapping flowerbeds.
we are flowers in a garden that isn't ours,
some bathe in the sun
whilst some of us bloom
comfortably in the shadows.

words of convenience

can up the pity; lid on tight.
enough to stop stale air escaping
and to never be able to remove it without aid.

erase bad will, thoughts and demons.
make way for truth, or,
stories—whichever works.

kill ugliness, as happiness
unfolds from the sheets
of forget
and joy comes
on the wings of creation.
and not in submission to those things...
we should leave behind.

pub parrot

I'm a caged, multi-coloured spy.
drunkard's mimic—'arse!'
barmaid's pet,
window dressing to a car park.
an interrupter,
foul-mouthed,
colourful.
shitting with a 'ding' of my cage.
hearing everything,
flying nowhere.

set me free.
you go to the pub when you fancy a drop.
I'm trapped,
a feathered clown—
and my drops 'ding'.

bittersweet

wry smiles
as the subtlest of blades takes the last
of the poison.
visitors from past lives bring gifts, hope.
when I'm out, I'll thank them. although will
be so changed they won't know me.
survival's hard, robbing what you thought
you were living for.

now I've survived and exist again, they can't
see anything but the poison—even though
it's gone, and what they thought was me
with it.

strength in sour smiles,
happiness in tears of disbelief.
I'm alive,
take solace, reflect.
for now, you are too.

can't get up

May beckons after months in the dark
any day soon a crack will show
neon lights splitting through, feeding
insatiable needs for rays;
calm waves after endless storms.

deep down in the sheets
empty thoughts
pained in the void.
runaway craziness;
escaping realities.
suffering disconnects,
stillborn happiness,
in every breath.
onwards we go for others though
now, get the hell out of bed.

crack of thunder
(deep in your eyes)

down darkened paths
endless pains
endless light
please, hold on.

in times forgotten and
now,

you are everything
or nothing
utopia in the stars
red rivers of pain too.

eyes to
your soul
eyes to horizons
seeing up and down spirals of life.

delete and re-write

I saw a memory replayed
uncertain if it was real.
a dream,
a suggestion.
in part
unsure,
if it happened at all.

the hurt and confusion felt real enough
as did the shame and
affect on me today.

then,
I realised
how little it matters
we're all reconstructed deconstructions
thoughts
reinterpreted.
suiting our confidence
egos
visions of ourselves and
a way ahead.

I now press delete on all those
bitter twangs.
boxing them up in a cupboard to be forgotten

letting the harmonies ring
beauty in single notes.
happiness is a story
we choose to tell—
sadness also,
if we open the box.

jumping out of trees

raiding factory bins to sell reject crystals at
school
running away,
getting caught.
homesickness, rock-laden stomach
uncontrollable tears of abandon.

jumping from a cliff into icy waters,
a witches' circle,
hay bales, rats in tunnels
sleepwalking in the rain,
murder in the dark.
Neighbours before Nightmare On Elm Street,
missing home,
a secret tear or two.

carried to school through 6ft of snow
by an ex-SAS soldier.
playing pirates,
setting traps in the woods to catch rabbits,
and lines to catch eels.

a first kiss,
posters of motorbikes out of reach,
friends in lockers, hanging on belts,
ketchup squirting on a master's sleeve,

bean bag frogs,
campervans.

climbing on rooftops,
raiding an abandoned farm like it's a secret
mission,
running away, again
getting caught, again
homesick, again.
— a tear.

sliding out of giant fern trees
UFOs,
missing home,
one less tear,
packing bags,
sitting on window ledges,
flicking bluebottles to die,
lost on misty wet moors,
pinning a bully against a wall,
never seeing him again.
missing home less and less,
no tears.

and all before the first real shave.

a new hope

answers to questions never asked.

new horizons burned,
every maker broken,
we toil for invisible monsters.

have we died again?
or, been born once over?
please forgive me this sad one,
everybody burns.

christmas

a Bristol girl wishes it came with sparkles,
barely afloat in the channel,
another is grateful to see land.

—

a boy in Manchester is sad it broke already
and Daddy's glue's ran out.
in Ukraine, a lad pulls mud from the stock,
blows the mechanism clear.
If it jams, he fixes it.
or, today he surely dies,
or is captured.

—

a parent in the big smoke wishes they'd
drunk less during the year and had more to
wrap.
another on the outskirts, high up in a tower,
wishes they had more to drink to forget the
year and another wrap to dull the din.

—

a writer longs for the perfect line,
to hit a transcendent chord.

a reader thinks they could do better,
they can,
you will.

lead weight

groundhog visions,
heavy head.

force feed,
force drink.

move because you have to
get up and get out—
over and over.

purpose drives the bones to dust,
as
responsibility blisters
tired eyes.
'till the weekend.
reset,
rewind,
imagining another way of living
spending the groundhog's gains.

penance for marriage
to
the system born into
not chosen.

then, start over again
up and beaten down under those

groundhog visions with waning
smiles this time.

as the sun glints off the road,
knowing there're only another five
days until
we're free again.

a glass of joy

pulsing temples
and uneven beats
from
liquid forced pleasures
to escape the storm.
a hard breakfast of headlines
and
political snipes bring thirst again.

—live a precious moment,

beauty in a breath of air,
a drink,
before the sun is straight up.

looking up
through
an emptied glass.
a lens to hope
mask reality.
draining funds that could
make for a real escape.

with the glass comes words,
a conspiring friend:
finish up,
buy a ticket,

hit the tracks,
forget the news,

—let's make our own.

hit parade

a small boy hands his Nan a cassette.
snap goes the VW's player:
swallows it, the last chocolate on earth.
seconds later,
she's head bobbing to Nirvana like they're
a cushion-clad crooner
on a pier end.

later, comes Soundgarden,
Sonic Youth and Pearl Jam.

she nods,
he smiles.

before he leaves for uni' she hands him a
cassette,
he stows it next to
Oasis
and
The Stone Roses.

he listens to her tape in secret,
as flatmates celebrate their choices so all can
hear
through vibrating walls.

only he can hear the Bach.

smiling,
head bobbing,
like he's in an old VW with Nirvana
and Nan.

road to nowhere (m4)

Eastbound:

he does it for the money
half asleep at the wheel
another insipid interaction
and
another tank of fuel
another jam
beige zombie-filled service station
money earned over many days
feeling like years
eventually holidaying Westbound
over days that feel like hours

Westbound:

they need a break
so do the kids
back seats chorus: I'm hungry.'
deflated wheezes from the front: 'there's
nothing left.'
'I'm hungry.'
10 miles on...
'I'm hungry.'
'There's one biscuit left, you'll have to share.'
'I'm hungry.'

'You'll have to wait until we cross the big
bridge.'
'I'm hungry.'
'fine, here you go. the last one. no more left.'
another 100 miles to go
six magical biscuits in reserve
they need a break
less the kids
or with
more biscuits

Eastbound:

he bought it to look flash
but only sees it when it's parked
inside, it's plastic
pretty much like the rest
the more miles he does
the less it matters
after all
he gets stuck in the same jams as the others
stops at the same pumps
shits and pisses in the same sorry stops
radio stations playing the same churn
regardless of the car's badge
it's when he's home it matters most
and he can't see it
but knows
the passers-by and neighbours can
they can't see him though
feet up, eyeing a huge TV
too big for the room

they can't see that either

Westbound:

there's a beach
a cliff
over a bridge to another country
if you work hard enough in the country
you're leaving

Eastbound:

there's an office
in a tower block
over a bridge to another country
if you can leave the land you love long
enough
to work the hours to afford the toll crossing

Westbound:

at the side of the road
Daddy's crow pecks at
a heap that used to be something
maybe a badger, deer or a fox
it's a long dangerous road, but
we've all gotta eat
right?

the trip

I took a trip down a darkening lane,
feeding
dead cold alleys and decrepit crusty doors.
walked through
thistled narrowing stabbing paths,
pulled on
in hope of light whilst
cut to the marrow.

the strain never eased,
frictions grew harder underfoot,
against arms
as I pushed through each challenge.

by the end,
rivulets of blood
trickled from the branches
and blistered sores burned ankles.
as I
turned to see
a way back in,
to relive the journey's pains over again,
and again.

that the thorny savage path
was a gift—

to feel,
have chances to return back over the barbed
path
a suffering suicidal miracle.

for if the trek gets easy,
it would be nothing at all,
like me.

daddy's crow watches...

always around a corner
in a tree
picking up a leaf
shitting on a car.
getting around
over
under
ontop
between things.

urban ghost
denizen of the trail
judge and jury.

sometimes in number
sometimes alone.

always there
breaking ice
defusing tantrums
raising smiles,
giggles
wonder.

majestic
pervasive warrior
noir prince(ss)

breaker-upper of rows
cawing witness
dear mascot to our adventures
fighting seagulls for the kids' scraps
never shitting on our car
always
the flashy one next along.

daddy's crow plays...

guitar, flute and Northumbrian pipes,
when you're not there.
he writes books, poetry and dead-end
screenplays too
in time that doesn't exist
he imagines things and gets them down
shares the best
keeps the worst to himself
it used to be the other way around.

Daddy's crow flies high
and low
capturing the best eavesdrops
and scenery for his prose
he combats himself too
internal fights full of woe
celebrates the high times too.

one day he'll pass the mantle
lookout
it could be to you.

grace

a man once passed, in a blink,
as if never with us.

lyrics lingered,
on the lips of tearful strangers,
veering near to their own cliff edges,
even in the darkest hope,
his words helped.

not everyone wept,
only the purest bloody angels.
telling a story
everyone heard,
whilst the precious few listened.

telling us of the man cut short
of his music.

Jeff's grace.
everlasting hopes left behind
for us all to feel
for us all to remember.

be here now,
understand pain.
clear way for broken souls,
keeping us afloat without water.

lighting the way
every bleeding heart sings true,
you can hear it on the wind.

look past the nail
in the wall

those rippled, distorted yesterdays,
held in a circle,
everyone owns the memory, scared to look.

mirrors: enemies to the present,
iridescent pains and scars,
reflected back at us.
relentless,
overly re-run moments,
relapses into dead seconds.

any dream will do—
lie bigger than the blackening glass before us.
wear, what it can't see:
a view to tomorrow's happy set piece,
yesterday's dead,
save it for when you are too.

lie flat,
imagine the blossom.
every tree has a chance,
so do those weeds like us.

belly up and smiling

bold knights resting on the bones of their friends,
killers killing over unanswered questions to false truths, ad's and rumour.
beaches filled with dead sea wonders, shipwrecks and stranded rotten whales.

dying stars flooding an empty space.
dogs running to an empty plate,
as minds, complex as interstellar infinity are quashed by groundhogs.
futures rush at the glimmer of hope
as pained pasts linger on forever.

a sorry moon sits heavy on the waves,
over those empty seas.
the last bird wails,
dunes echoing pain.
the bitter winds
whipping through our hair.
we take a drag
from the cigarette of life, without care.
the sands are harsh,
full of death and decay.
for in this moment,
we feel alive.

beautiful futility,
hope in the now.
savouring fresh smells on the wind,
that won't last—quickly passing.
the touch of lush bracken.

all this is:
rare temporal unique diamonds,
sparkling in the rough
constructs of our minds.

snake in the boardroom and king of the estate

arise from the ashes of a single mum's
barmaid's wages,
rise past the red bricks,
creosote on knees from climbing rooftops.
thick and thin-skinned
into yourself, into the
city.

monikers dropped,
on with the new skin and flesh.
now is the time to rise again,
knowing your past,
everyone is inequal
you know most of all,
some are more unequal than others.

nihilists and pen warriors unite,
or beer pump mumblers.
revellers of the night,
towards hope and change.
having more than yesterday, more than
even our mothers and fathers.
running from the past.
never forgetting.

guilty at change,
up until the paychecks drop.
inciting resentment and the starting blocks,
to the rear, back of the pack,
a race nearly lost before it began.
racing towards the rear.

wilting with the efforts,
always getting back up again.
remembering those who came before,
resemblances in the mirror.
inside of us,
or a
reckoning
summoned to break the mould.

the mirror

a tired old man said,
when he used to look in the mirror,
he no longer knew who looked back.
that the child had vanished,
that he never recognised
that either,
the reflection always painted a distorted
shell,
not the
shining nugget within.

he said, he used to walk the dog.
now it walks him.
take a drink,
now it takes a slice out of him
with each drop.

used to paint a picture,
now he's more in it, than wielding a brush.
he feels like a figment of the artist's strokes,
no longer the creator himself.

he said that, now, when he looks in the
mirror
he sees deep lines, a hundred journeys,
paved with

life-long friends.

and the mirror never saw those coming.
or, the heart still beating.

arm wrestle

life begins with a contest to survive,
then there's youth: days, with surging
energy, might,
burning spirits,
dreams scorched by approaching adulthood
we push on, seeking triumph and an
embrace to last longer than
a last order's call.

when our arm grows weary, and the wrestle
reaches an end,
we hope to look back without regret.
at a blown battlefield, a shattered arena of
existence.

life's an arm wrestle; sinews strained and
muscles flexed.
with victories not defined by raw power,
dominance, or undermined prowess.

with enduring twists and turns,
victory lies not in might,
but in that distilled burning spirit
as it echoes in what we've
left behind.

fleeting breaths

distant shores grow further
as hands we hold grow colder
with each stroke
evanescence and demise wait to greet us on a
blurring horizon,
as cataracts attack where our loved ones
starred.
once seeing the immortal,
now barely held together
dust.
the waves attack sea breaks, dunes and
shelters,
a glorious chorus
on sands that always shift,
skin that always ages.
a small boy leans into the wall of rain
screaming for lightning smiling at the
blackness,
for someday soon,
he'll be an old man.
across the bay, a girl stands proud against the
winds,
loving the feel of rain on her skin.
one day they might meet in the middle
before heading over the horizon

together.
don't mourn the passing fleet of children to
dust,
or cry as what's meant to go, will.
memories, grains and raindrops.
watering paths we sowed with each lasting
breath,
a trace,
death,
then grace.

Thank You

If you can spare a few minutes, please leave a review on Amazon and Goodreads.

Your thoughts will help like minded souls find these words.

About The Author

John Bowie

 John Bowie was born in Northumberland, Northern England and studied in Manchester in the '90s. He has published poetry, novels and short stories. He now lives in Bristol, U.K. John is the founder and editor-in-chief of Bristol Noir.

Also by John Bowie:

Poetry: Dead Birds & Sinking Ships, Walking towards The Noise

Novels: Untethered, Transference, Division, Viking, Weston-super-Nightmare

Featured in (Anthologies): Savage Minds & Raging Bulls, Tainted Hearts & Dirty Hell Hounds, Where Angels Fall, Gone

Poetry By John Bowie

Poetry collections in the spirit of Charles Bukowski, Sylvia Plath, Rupi Kaur, Sarah Kane and Ted Hughes. John Bowie's poetry collections are full of dirty realism, emotion, heart and soul.

Walking Towards The Noise

A collection of poems for those who feel life's complexities. Capturing times during lockdown and the memories we rely on to inform our decision-making through love, loss and facing up to life's challenges.

Dead Birds & Sinking Ships

A visceral relay of emotions from childhood in the country and growing old in the city. Exposing love, loss, hurt and wanting. Knowing death waits to deny us the people, places and events that make us.

Novels By John Bowie

As well as poetry collections, John Bowie has also written a series of crime noir thrillers.

'Set in 1998 in Bristol, England, Bowie's dark, hard-edged crime novel Untethered inaugurates a promising series'— Publishers Weekly

'Noir fans will find a lot to like' — BookLife

'...there are so many great writers that this book brings to mind: the dirty realism of Bukowski, Fante and McCarthy and the best noir writing from Raymond Chandler and James Ellroy' — Storgy magazine

Untethered: A Dark Hard-Edged Crime Noir Set In Bristol

CLASSIC CRIME NOIR FULL OF DIRTY REALISM SET IN '90s BRISTOL

A crime noir, reminiscent of old noir films like Chinatown and Double Indemnity full of dark humour. A disturbed ex-SAS soldier searches for meaning in alcohol as madness sets in and a series of cryptic messages arrive, pulling him into a web of deceit, destruction and disillusionment. With a knock on his door comes a chance to find a missing girl and start over again...as a private investigator.

'We were all puppets of someone in a self-perpetuating circle of pollutants, violence and hedonistic escapism.'—John Black, Untethered

Transference: A Brutal And Lyrical Manchester Crime Thriller

BRUTAL, DARK AND LYRICAL MANC NOIR

As clubbers in Manchester's most notorious club partied hard in the 90s, a girl collapsed, falling from the stage after a bad pill. Few noticed. Those that did, didn't care, lost in a hedonistic haze. John Black, an ex-SAS soldier, who was working security that night, carried her out in his arms. Now on witness protection for exposing the city's underworld after the girl's death, he returns to the city that disowned him. Helping a troubled mother search for answers to her son's suicide — as eerie recordings tell of increased sexual depravity in the block of flats he jumped from. Confronting the orchestrator of his pains, he works to solve the case, have vengeance... and reclaim his lost identity.

'Lyrical-poetry and prose mix with blood down Manchster's harsh rain-soaked alleyways.'

Division: A Violent Crime Thriller Set In Northumberland

DARKNESS FOLLOWS WHEREVER HE GOES

John Black returns to Northern England for a family funeral, having left the woman he loves to protect her from his past. His solace is broken as the sands shift, crows and gulls circle overhead, and children run on the beach where John used to play as a child... and where a body is found in the dunes by Cross Hill — the body of a woman John once knew. With a set of coordinates left for him in a haunted pub, the body count grows, and the police are made fully aware of John's connection. As he drives the ancient coastal and rural landscapes, from Alnwick Castle, Hadrian's Wall, Cragside to Kielder, racing to confront the killers, John wrestles the pain of bringing the evils of his past to his homelands and to all who know him.

Viking: A Fast-Paced Action Noir In The Jungles Of Malaysia

A NEO-NOIR HONEYMOON IN HELL

He thought he'd given up the drinking...and the killing. Ghosts haunt John and Cherry's honeymoon escape in the jungles of Malaysia and Borneo as the release of nihilist criminals linked to John's SAS past triggers death and destruction back home. When their luxury island resort is raided by savage pirates, it's clear everything is connected and they can't hide from destiny. To love, hate—kill or be killed. And most of all, the ghosts are as real as they are. Past, present and future violently collide as they realise they're forever trapped in a matrix of fate. To love, hate, kill...repeat.

Weston-Super-Nightmare: A Hellbent Riff Raff Thriller

A CLASSIC PULP NOIR (in Weston)

The Hell's Belles was Jimi's bar. A retirement gift to himself after a hard life's graft and no one owned the stage but him and his Gibson SG – except ex-strippers, Tammy and Betty. Matt, the youngest brother to three of The South Bank Cricketers, the infamous London gang, wanted to play – not gonna happen. Jimi needed backup. He knew some gangsters of his own, and had criminal friends. But that's not who he was going to call. He needed something tougher, more reliable... made of stone.

Printed in Great Britain
by Amazon

26355640R00078